BIBLE PUZZLES

CROSSWORDS

Authors .... *Roy J. Nichols*
Monte Corley

Cover Design .... *Gary Zupkas*

For information regarding the CPSIA on this printed material call: 203-595-3636 and provide reference # LANC-315751

Copyright ©2010 • Twenty Second Printing
Rainbow Publishers • P.O. Box 261129 • San Diego, CA 92196
www.rainbowpublishers.com

SUSTAINABLE FORESTRY INITIATIVE

Certified Chain of Custody
Promoting Sustainable
Forest Management
www.sfiprogram.org

#RB36151
ISBN 10: 0-937282-51-0
ISBN 13: 978-0-937282-51-9

RELIGION / Christian Ministry / Children

CONTENTS

INTRODUCTION

The exciting puzzles contained in this *Bible Puzzles* book will bring new fun and enthusiasm to the learning and reviewing of Bible facts and the development of Bible-use skills. The individual puzzle sheets can be used for readiness, reinforcement and review activities, and for enrichment in the Bible class and at home.

Each of the four books in the *Bible Puzzles* series provides a variety of puzzles for children ages 8 through 13 (but older teens and adults will enjoy many of the puzzles too!). Individual puzzles may be duplicated for use with groups. Answers are provided on the back of each puzzle.

The King James Version of the Bible is the biblical reference for the puzzles.

1
BIBLE CHARACTERS
CROSSWORDS

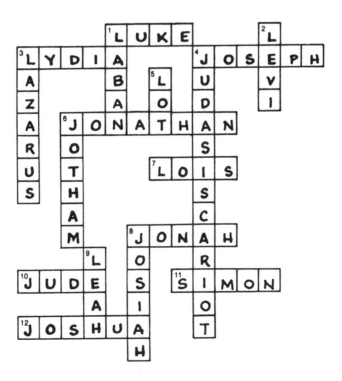

BIBLE CHARACTERS
BAASHA TO BOAZ

ACROSS

1. Youngest son of Jacob (Gen. 35:16-18)
2. A robber and murderer (Mark 15:7)
6. Wife of David and mother of Solomon
   (1 Kings 1:11)
7. A disobedient prophet (Num. 22:1-22)
8. King of Israel who fought Asa (1 Kings 15:16)
9. Blind beggar of Jericho (Mark 10:46)

DOWN

1. Helped free Israel from Jabin (Judg. 4:6-8)
3. One of the twelve apostles (Matt. 10:3)
4. Missionary companion of Paul (Acts 13:2)
5. Last king of Babylon (Dan. 5)
6. Married Ruth (Ruth 4:13)

BIBLE CHARACTERS
BAASHA TO BOAZ

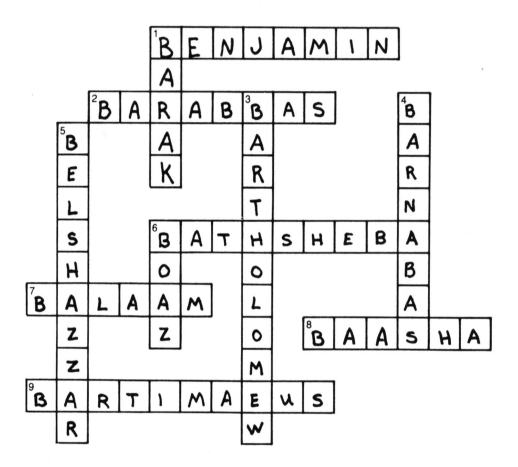

ACROSS

1. Youngest son of Jacob (Gen. 35:16-18)
2. A robber and murderer (Mark 15:7)
6. Wife of David and mother of Solomon (1 Kings 1:11)
7. A disobedient prophet (Num. 22:1-22)
8. King of Israel who fought Asa (1 Kings 15:16)
9. Blind beggar of Jericho (Mark 10:46)

DOWN

1. Helped free Israel from Jabin (Judg. 4:6-8)
3. One of the twelve apostles (Matt. 10:3)
4. Missionary companion of Paul (Acts 13:2)
5. Last king of Babylon (Dan. 5)
6. Married Ruth (Ruth 4:13)

BIBLE CHARACTERS
CAIAPHAS TO DORCAS

ACROSS

1. Another name for Simon Peter (John 1:42)
3. A Christian full of good works (Acts 9:36)
5. A Persian king (Ezra 4:24)
6. Ruler of a synagogue in Corinth (Acts 18:8)
8. The fourth major prophet (Ezekiel 14:14-20)
10. A Philistine woman (Judges 16)
12. A New Testament high priest (Matt. 26:3)
13. The fifth son of Jacob (Gen. 30:6)

DOWN

1. A Persian king (Ezra 1:1-7)
2. Second king of Israel (2 Sam. 5:1-4)
4. A Roman soldier (Acts 10)
7. A prophetess and judge (Judg. 4:4-24)
9. One of the twelve spies (Num. 14:6-10)
11. The oldest son of Adam (Gen. 4)

BIBLE CHARACTERS
CAIAPHAS TO DORCAS

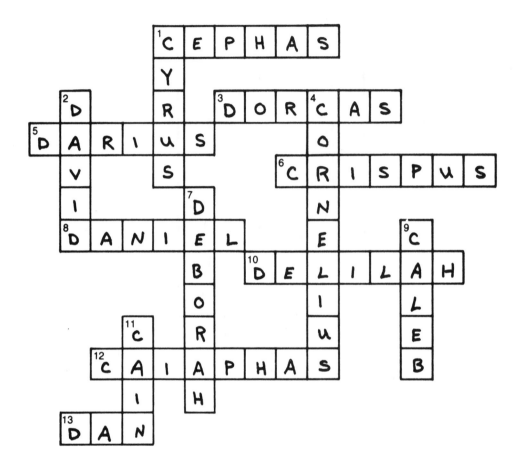

ACROSS
1. Another name for Simon Peter (John 1:42)
3. A Christian full of good works (Acts 9:36)
5. A Persian king (Ezra 4:24)
6. Ruler of a synagogue in Corinth (Acts 18:8)
8. The fourth major prophet (Ezekiel 14:14-20)
10. A Philistine woman (Judges 16)
12. A New Testament high priest (Matt. 26:3)
13. The fifth son of Jacob (Gen. 30:6)

DOWN
1. A Persian king (Ezra 1:1-7)
2. Second king of Israel (2 Sam. 5:1-4)
4. A Roman soldier (Acts 10)
7. A prophetess and judge (Judg. 4:4-24)
9. One of the twelve spies (Num. 14:6-10)
11. The oldest son of Adam (Gen. 4)

14

BIBLE CHARACTERS
EHUD TO EZRA

ACROSS

4. A prophet who was fed by ravens (1 Kings 17:1-7)
5. A prophet during the exile of Israel (Ezek. 1:3)
6. A priest during the time of Joshua (Josh. 14:1)
7. First woman created by God (Gen. 3:20)
9. Mother of Timothy (2 Tim. 1:5)
10. A righteous man who did not die (Gen. 5:24)
11. A queen who saved her people (Esth. 3–5)
12. Second judge of Israel (Judg. 3:12-30)

DOWN

1. Prophet who cured Naaman's leprosy (2 Kings 5:1-14)
2. An evil king of Israel killed by Zimri (1 Kings 16:6-14)
3. Priest who trained Samuel (1 Sam. 3:1-18)
4. Mother of John the Baptist (Luke 1:5-57)
7. Judged Israel ten years. (Judg. 12:11, 12)
8. One of the sons of Joseph born in Egypt (Gen. 46:20)
9. Oldest and favorite son of Isaac (Gen. 25:24-28)
10. A priest during the exile (Neh. 8:1-8)

BIBLE CHARACTERS
EHUD TO EZRA

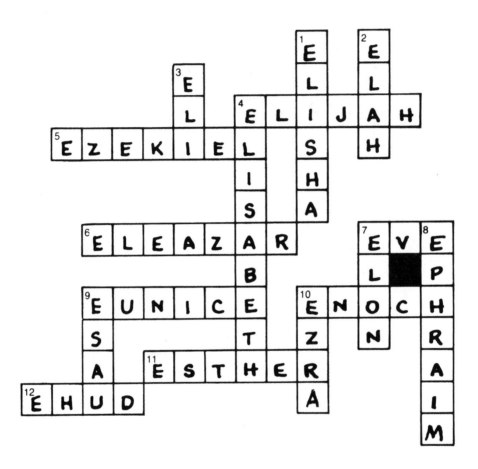

ACROSS

4. A prophet who was fed by ravens
   (1 Kings 17:1-7)
5. A prophet during the exile of Israel
   (Ezek. 1:3)
6. A priest during the time of Joshua
   (Josh. 14:1)
7. First woman created by God (Gen. 3:20)
9. Mother of Timothy (2 Tim. 1:5)
10. A righteous man who did not die (Gen. 5:24)
11. A queen who saved her people (Esth. 3–5)
12. Second judge of Israel (Judg. 3:12-30)

DOWN

1. Prophet who cured Naaman's leprosy
   (2 Kings 5:1-14)
2. An evil king of Israel killed by Zimri
   (1 Kings 16:6-14)
3. Priest who trained Samuel (1 Sam. 3:1-18)
4. Mother of John the Baptist (Luke 1:5-57)
7. Judged Israel ten years. (Judg. 12:11, 12)
8. One of the sons of Joseph born in Egypt
   (Gen. 46:20)
9. Oldest and favorite son of Isaac
   (Gen. 25:24-28)
10. A priest during the exile (Neh. 8:1-8)

BIBLE CHARACTERS
FELIX TO HOSHEA

ACROSS

3. A good king of Judah (2 Chron. 29:1-11)
5. Mother of Ishmael (Gen. 16:15, 16)
7. Mother of Samuel (1 Sam. 1:20-28)
9. Governor of Judea after Felix (Acts 25:1)
11. Paul's Jewish teacher (Acts 22:3)
12. Fought with a horn, jar, and lamp (Judg. 7:15-23)

DOWN

1. The Great; killed the children of Bethlehem (Matt. 2)
2. King of Tyre (1 Kings 5:1)
3. A minor prophet (Hab. 1:1-4)
4. Last king of Israel (2 Kings 17:1-6)
6. Minor prophet after the captivity (Hag. 1:1-4)
8. First of minor prophets (Hos. 1:1)
9. Governor of Judea (Acts 23:26)
10. Philistine giant (1 Sam. 17:4)
11. The seventh son of Jacob (Gen. 30:11)

BIBLE CHARACTERS
FELIX TO HOSHEA

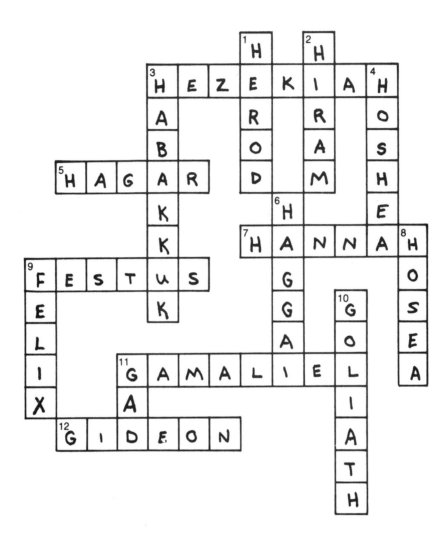

ACROSS

3. A good king of Judah (2 Chron. 29:1-11)
5. Mother of Ishmael (Gen. 16:15, 16)
7. Mother of Samuel (1 Sam. 1:20-28)
9. Governor of Judea after Felix (Acts 25:1)
11. Paul's Jewish teacher (Acts 22:3)
12. Fought with a horn, jar, and lamp
    (Judg. 7:15-23)

DOWN

1. The Great; killed the children of Bethlehem
   (Matt. 2)
2. King of Tyre (1 Kings 5:1)
3. A minor prophet (Hab. 1:1-4)
4. Last king of Israel (2 Kings 17:1-6)
6. Minor prophet after the captivity (Hag. 1:1-4)
8. First of minor prophets (Hos. 1:1)
9. Governor of Judea (Acts 23:26)
10. Philistine giant (1 Sam. 17:4)
11. The seventh son of Jacob (Gen. 30:11)

BIBLE CHARACTERS
IBZAN TO JEREMIAH

ACROSS

1. A captain in Israel's army when Elisha appointed him king (2 Kings 9:11-12)
3. Son of Josiah, King of Judah (2 Kings 23:34-37)
5. King of Judah who surrendered to Nebuchadnezzar (Jer. 52:31-34)
7. The ninth son of Jacob (Gen. 30:18)
9. Brother of Esau and father of twelve tribes of Israel (Gen. 28:10-17)
11. One of twelve apostles, brother of John (Matt. 4:21, 22)
13. King of Israel seventeen years (2 Kings 13:1-9)
14. Half brother of Isaac, older son of Abraham (Gen. 17:18-22)
15. Prophet of Judah; foretold coming of Christ (2 Kings 19:2; Isaiah 9:6)

DOWN

1. Judge of Israel twenty-two years (Judg. 10:3-5)
2. Judged Israel six years; defeated the Ammonites (Judg. 11-12)
3. Son of Asa, a good king of Judah (2 Chron. 17:1-6)
4. Son of Abraham and Sarah (Gen. 21:1-5)
5. Name of kings in both Israel and Judah (1 Kings 22:50; 2 Kings 1:17)
6. Son of Hilkiah, prophet in Judah (Jer. 1:1, 2)
8. Name given to Jacob by God (Gen. 32:24-29)
10. Judged Israel for seven years after Jephthah (Judges 12:8-10)
11. Eldest of Job's three daughters (Job 42:14)
12. Jesus raised this man's daughter from the dead (Mark 5:22-42).

BIBLE CHARACTERS
IBZAN TO JEREMIAH

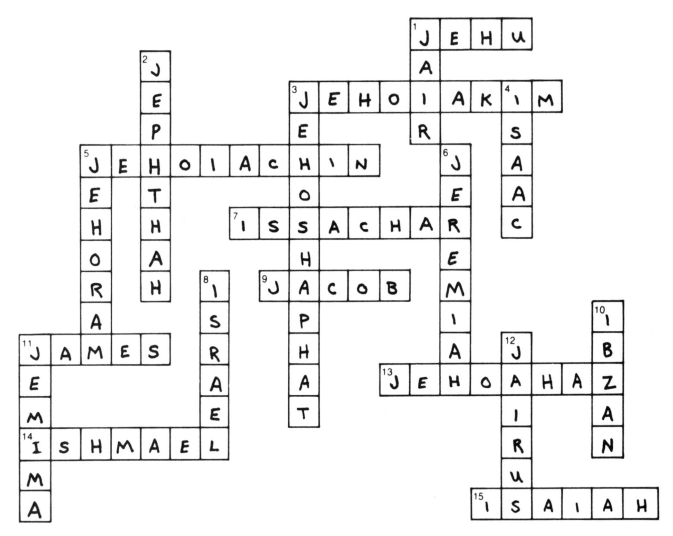

ACROSS

1. A captain in Israel's army when Elisha appointed him king (2 Kings 9:11-12)
3. Son of Josiah, King of Judah (2 Kings 23:34-37)
5. King of Judah who surrendered to Nebuchadnezzar (Jer. 52:31-34)
7. The ninth son of Jacob (Gen. 30:18)
9. Brother of Esau and father of twelve tribes of Israel (Gen. 28:10-17)
11. One of twelve apostles, brother of John (Matt. 4:21, 22)
13. King of Israel seventeen years (2 Kings 13:1-9)
14. Half brother of Isaac, older son of Abraham (Gen. 17:18-22)
15. Prophet of Judah; foretold coming of Christ (2 Kings 19:2; Isaiah 9:6)

DOWN

1. Judge of Israel twenty-two years (Judg. 10:3-5)
2. Judged Israel six years; defeated the Ammonites (Judg. 11-12)
3. Son of Asa, a good king of Judah (2 Chron. 17:1-6)
4. Son of Abraham and Sarah (Gen. 21:1-5)
5. Name of kings in both Israel and Judah (1 Kings 22:50; 2 Kings 1:17)
6. Son of Hilkiah, prophet in Judah (Jer. 1:1, 2)
8. Name given to Jacob by God (Gen. 32:24-29)
10. Judged Israel for seven years after Jephthah (Judges 12:8-10)
11. Eldest of Job's three daughters (Job 42:14)
12. Jesus raised this man's daughter from the dead (Mark 5:22-42).

BIBLE CHARACTERS
JEROBOAM TO JUDE

ACROSS

2. Both Israel and Judah had kings with this name (2 Kings 14:1; 13:10)
5. Old Testament prophet; oldest son of Samuel; (Joel 1:1; 1 Sam. 8:2)
6. The Good Shepherd (John 10:11-18)
7. He baptized Jesus (Matt. 3:1, 13-17)
8. The fourth son of Jacob and Leah (Gen. 35:22, 23)
9. Swallowed by a big fish (Jon. 1:11–2:10)
10. Led the Hebrews across the Jordan (Josh. 1:1, 2)
11. New Testament book before Revelation
12. Faithful in suffering (Job 2:3)

DOWN

1. Father of David (1 Samuel 16:6-13)
2. Friend of David (1 Sam. 20)
3. Brother of James (Matt. 4:21)
4. Jacob's son sold into slavery (Gen. 37:23-36)
6. King of Judah at age eight (2 Kings 22:1)
7. First king of the ten tribes of Israel (1 Kings 12:20)
8. Father of King Ahaz (2 Chron. 27:1-9)
9. Betrayed Jesus (Matt. 27:3-4)
11. General of King David's army (1 Chron. 27:34)

BIBLE CHARACTERS
JEROBOAM TO JUDE

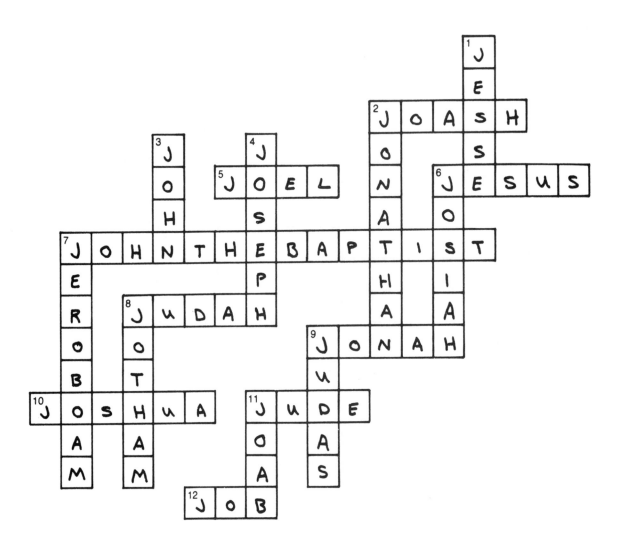

ACROSS

2. Both Israel and Judah had kings with this name (2 Kings 14:1; 13:10)
5. Old Testament prophet; oldest son of Samuel; (Joel 1:1; 1 Sam. 8:2)
6. The Good Shepherd (John 10:11-18)
7. He baptized Jesus (Matt. 3:1, 13-17)
8. The fourth son of Jacob and Leah (Gen. 35:22, 23)
9. Swallowed by a big fish (Jon. 1:11–2:10)
10. Led the Hebrews across the Jordan (Josh. 1:1, 2)
11. New Testament book before Revelation
12. Faithful in suffering (Job 2:3)

DOWN

1. Father of David (1 Samuel 16:6-13)
2. Friend of David (1 Sam. 20)
3. Brother of James (Matt. 4:21)
4. Jacob's son sold into slavery (Gen. 37:23-36)
6. King of Judah at age eight (2 Kings 22:1)
7. First king of the ten tribes of Israel (1 Kings 12:20)
8. Father of King Ahaz (2 Chron. 27:1-9)
9. Betrayed Jesus (Matt. 27:3-4)
11. General of King David's army (1 Chron. 27:34)

BIBLE CHARACTERS
KORAH TO MOSES

ACROSS

1. Saved Jews from Haman's plot (Esth. 3:5-6; 4)
2. A physician (Col. 4:14)
3. Priest and king of Salem (Gen. 14:17-20)
6. Led Israel from Egypt (Exod. 6:1-8)
7. Oldest son of Joseph (Gen. 41:51)
10. Nephew of Abraham (Gen. 11:27, 31)
11. First convert in Philippi (Acts 16:14, 15, 40)
12. Sixth of minor prophets (Jer. 26:18)
15. Sister of Mary and Lazarus (Luke 10:38)
16. Father-in-law of Jacob (Gen. 29:13-16)
17. One of three in fiery furnace (Dan. 3:19-20)
19. Sister of Aaron (Exod. 15:20)
20. Mother of Jesus (Matt. 1:18-25)

DOWN

1. Lived 969 years (Gen. 5:25-27)
4. Conspired against Moses and Aaron (Num. 16:1-32)
5. Third son of Jacob and Leah (Gen. 29:34)
7. Chosen to replace Judas (Acts 1:23, 26)
8. First wife of David (1 Sam. 18:20-21)
9. Jesus raised him from the dead (John 11:5-44)
10. Grandmother of Timothy (2 Tim. 1:5)
12. A tax collector called to be an apostle (Matt. 9:9)
13. Daughter of Laban (Gen. 29:16)
14. Last book of the Old Testament
17. First name was John (Acts 12:12, 25)
18. A name meaning "bitter" (Ruth 1:20)

BIBLE CHARACTERS
KORAH TO MOSES

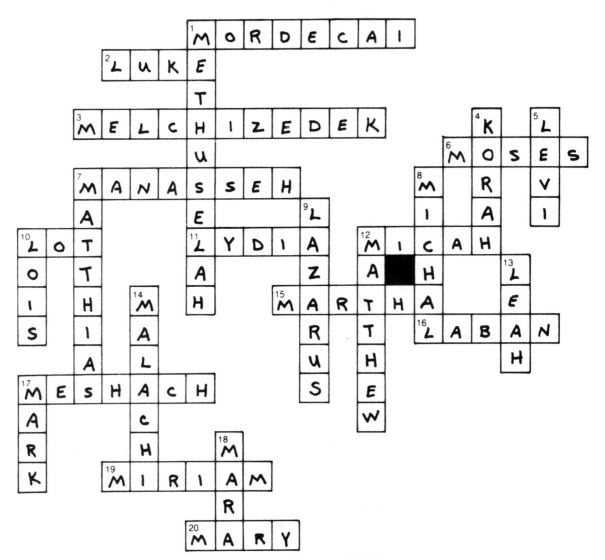

ACROSS

1. Saved Jews from Haman's plot (Esth. 3:5-6; 4)
2. A physician (Col. 4:14)
3. Priest and king of Salem (Gen. 14:17-20)
6. Led Israel from Egypt (Exod. 6:1-8)
7. Oldest son of Joseph (Gen. 41:51)
10. Nephew of Abraham (Gen. 11:27, 31)
11. First convert in Philippi (Acts 16:14, 15, 40)
12. Sixth of minor prophets (Jer. 26:18)
15. Sister of Mary and Lazarus (Luke 10:38)
16. Father-in-law of Jacob (Gen. 29:13-16)
17. One of three in fiery furnace (Dan. 3:19-20)
19. Sister of Aaron (Exod. 15:20)
20. Mother of Jesus (Matt. 1:18-25)

DOWN

1. Lived 969 years (Gen. 5:25-27)
4. Conspired against Moses and Aaron (Num. 16:1-32)
5. Third son of Jacob and Leah (Gen. 29:34)
7. Chosen to replace Judas (Acts 1:23, 26)
8. First wife of David (1 Sam. 18:20-21)
9. Jesus raised him from the dead (John 11:5-44)
10. Grandmother of Timothy (2 Tim. 1:5)
12. A tax collector called to be an apostle (Matt. 9:9)
13. Daughter of Laban (Gen. 29:16)
14. Last book of the Old Testament
17. First name was John (Acts 12:12, 25)
18. A name meaning "bitter" (Ruth 1:20)

BIBLE CHARACTERS
NAAMAN TO OTHNIEL

ACROSS

2. Sixth son of Jacob (Gen. 30:8)
4. Builder of Samaria (1 Kings 16:23-28)
5. A disciple without guile (John 1:47)
7. Owned a vineyard (1 Kings 21:1)
8. Prophesied against Nineveh (Nah. 1:1)
12. A runaway slave (Philem. 1:10-19)
13. Rebuilder of Jerusalem's walls
    (Neh. 1:1; 2:17-4:23)
14. Prophet and advisor to David (2 Sam. 7:2, 3)

DOWN

1. Mother-in-law of Ruth (Ruth 1:1-4)
3. A Syrian leper (2 Kings 5:1-14)
5. Daniel explained his dream (Dan. 4:18-27)
6. A judge of Israel (Judg. 3:9-11)
9. Builder of the ark (Gen. 7)
10. Came to Jesus by night (John 3:1-21)
11. Shortest book in the Old Testament

BIBLE CHARACTERS
NAAMAN TO OTHNIEL

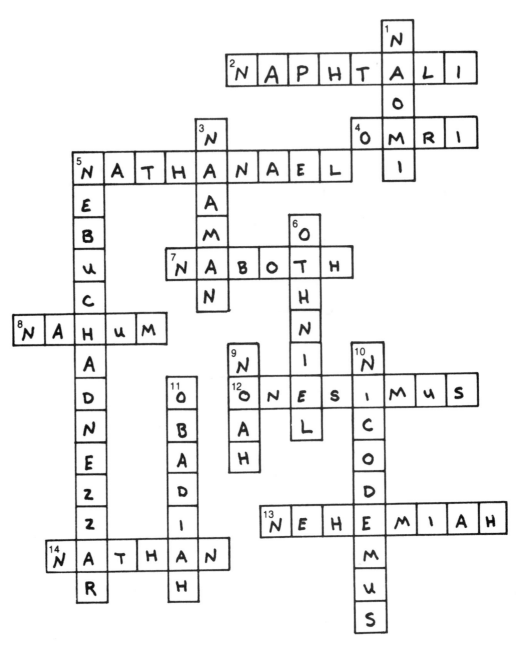

ACROSS

2. Sixth son of Jacob (Gen. 30:8)
4. Builder of Samaria (1 Kings 16:23-28)
5. A disciple without guile (John 1:47)
7. Owned a vineyard (1 Kings 21:1)
8. Prophesied against Nineveh (Nah. 1:1)
12. A runaway slave (Philem. 1:10-19)
13. Rebuilder of Jerusalem's walls (Neh. 1:1; 2:17-4:23)
14. Prophet and advisor to David (2 Sam. 7:2, 3)

DOWN

1. Mother-in-law of Ruth (Ruth 1:1-4)
3. A Syrian leper (2 Kings 5:1-14)
5. Daniel explained his dream (Dan. 4:18-27)
6. A judge of Israel (Judg. 3:9-11)
9. Builder of the ark (Gen. 7)
10. Came to Jesus by night (John 3:1-21)
11. Shortest book in the Old Testament

BIBLE CHARACTERS
PAUL TO RUTH

ACROSS

5. King of Judah; killed by Pekah (2 Kings 15:22-26)
7. Wife of Isaac (Gen. 24:67)
8. Egyptian official (Gen. 37:36)
9. A Moabite widow (Book of Ruth)
10. Had a slave called Onesimus (Philem. 1:1, 10-19)
11. Roman governor of Judea (Matt. 27:2-65)

DOWN

1. Ruled Israel twenty years (2 Kings 15:27)
2. An apostle from Bethsaida (John 1:43-44)
3. Title for kings of Egypt (Gen. 41:46)
4. Oldest son of Jacob (Gen. 29:32)
6. Wife of Jacob (Gen. 29:18)
7. King after Solomon (1 Kings 11:43)
8. Also called Saul; made three missionary journeys (Acts 13:2, 9)
10. First a fisherman, then an apostle (Luke 5:1-11)

BIBLE CHARACTERS
PAUL TO RUTH

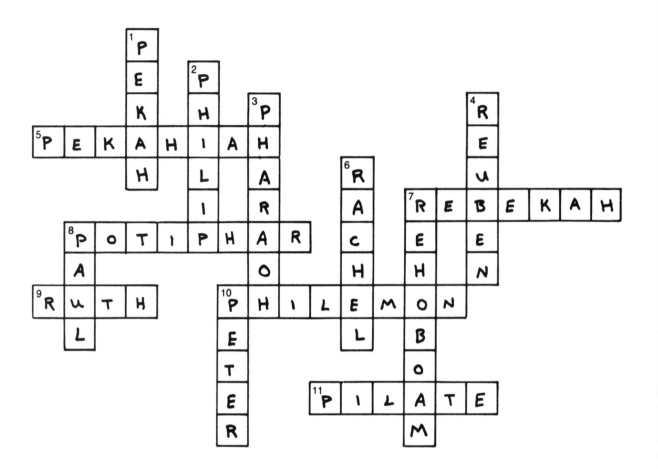

ACROSS

5. King of Judah; killed by Pekah
   (2 Kings 15:22-26)
7. Wife of Isaac (Gen. 24:67)
8. Egyptian official (Gen. 37:36)
9. A Moabite widow (Book of Ruth)
10. Had a slave called Onesimus (Philem. 1:1, 10-19)
11. Roman governor of Judea (Matt. 27:2-65)

DOWN

1. Ruled Israel twenty years (2 Kings 15:27)
2. An apostle from Bethsaida (John 1:43-44)
3. Title for kings of Egypt (Gen. 41:46)
4. Oldest son of Jacob (Gen. 29:32)
6. Wife of Jacob (Gen. 29:18)
7. King after Solomon (1 Kings 11:43)
8. Also called Saul; made three missionary journeys (Acts 13:2, 9)
10. First a fisherman, then an apostle (Luke 5:1-11)

BIBLE CHARACTERS
SALOME TO STEPHEN

ACROSS
1. Anointed King David (1 Sam. 16:1-13)
2. Destroyed a pagan temple (Judg. 16:21-31)
6. Wife of Abraham (Gen. 17:15-19)
7. Assyrian king who invaded Judah (2 Kings 19:20)
9. One of Noah's sons (Gen. 5:32)
10. King for a month (2 Kings 15:10-15)
12. Told a lie and died (Acts 5:1-11)
13. Known for his wisdom (1 Kings 3:5-12)

DOWN
1. A zealot and a disciple (Luke 6:15)
2. Cast into Nebuchadnezzar's furnace (Dan. 3:19)
3. Companion of Paul (Acts 16:19-40)
4. Third son of Adam (Gen. 4:25)
5. One of women who served Jesus (Mark 16:1-8)
7. Stoned to death (Acts 7:54-60)
8. Killed 600 Philistines (Judg. 3:31)
10. Second son of Jacob (Gen. 29:33)
11. First king of Israel (1 Sam. 9:25–10:1)

BIBLE CHARACTERS
SALOME TO STEPHEN

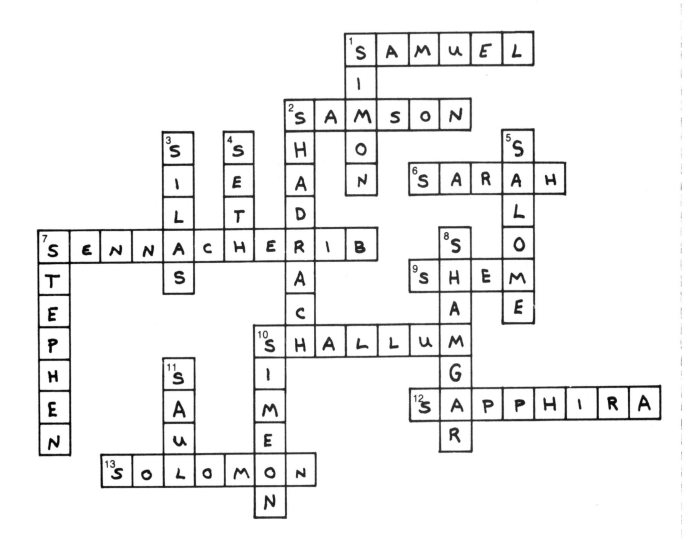

ACROSS

1. Anointed King David (1 Sam. 16:1-13)
2. Destroyed a pagan temple (Judg. 16:21-31)
6. Wife of Abraham (Gen. 17:15-19)
7. Assyrian king who invaded Judah (2 Kings 19:20)
9. One of Noah's sons (Gen. 5:32)
10. King for a month (2 Kings 15:10-15)
12. Told a lie and died (Acts 5:1-11)
13. Known for his wisdom (1 Kings 3:5-12)

DOWN

1. A zealot and a disciple (Luke 6:15)
2. Cast into Nebuchadnezzar's furnace (Dan. 3:19)
3. Companion of Paul (Acts 16:19-40)
4. Third son of Adam (Gen. 4:25)
5. One of women who served Jesus (Mark 16:1-8)
7. Stoned to death (Acts 7:54-60)
8. Killed 600 Philistines (Judg. 3:31)
10. Second son of Jacob (Gen. 29:33)
11. First king of Israel (1 Sam. 9:25–10:1)

BIBLE CHARACTERS
THADDAEUS TO ZIMRI

ACROSS

3. A judge of Israel (Judg. 10:1, 2)
4. Father of James and John (Matt. 4:21)
5. A prince of Judah who helped to rebuild the temple (Ezra 5:2)
6. Young preacher from Lystra (Acts 16:1)
7. David took his wife (2 Sam. 11:26, 27)
9. Another name for Judas (not Iscariot) (Matt. 10:3)
10. A Greek Christian and a New Testament book (Gal. 2:1-3)
11. Climbed a tree to see Jesus (Luke 19:1-10)
12. A queen of Persia (Esth. 1:10-12)
13. Ruled Israel seven days after killing King Elah (1 Kings 16:9-20)
14. A king in Judah fifty-two years (2 Chron. 26:1-3)

DOWN

1. The tenth son of Jacob (Gen. 30:20)
2. Revolted against Nebuchadnezzar (2 Kings 24:20)
3. Book of Acts is addressed to him (Acts 1:1)
5. Father of John the Baptist (Luke 1:5-23)
6. Sometimes known as the doubter (John 20:24-29)
8. Ninth of the minor prophets (Zeph. 1:1)

BIBLE CHARACTERS
THADDAEUS TO ZIMRI

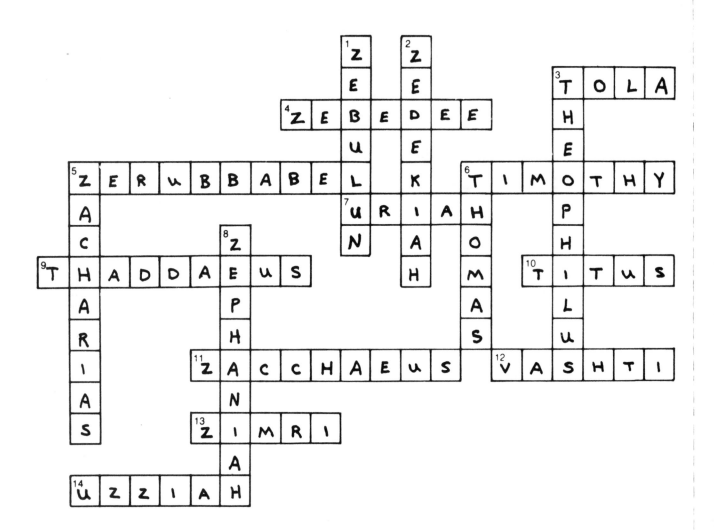

ACROSS

3. A judge of Israel (Judg. 10:1, 2)
4. Father of James and John (Matt. 4:21)
5. A prince of Judah who helped to rebuild the temple (Ezra 5:2)
6. Young preacher from Lystra (Acts 16:1)
7. David took his wife (2 Sam. 11:26, 27)
9. Another name for Judas (not Iscariot) (Matt. 10:3)
10. A Greek Christian and a New Testament book (Gal. 2:1-3)
11. Climbed a tree to see Jesus (Luke 19:1-10)
12. A queen of Persia (Esth. 1:10-12)
13. Ruled Israel seven days after killing King Elah (1 Kings 16:9-20)
14. A king in Judah fifty-two years (2 Chron. 26:1-3)

DOWN

1. The tenth son of Jacob (Gen. 30:20)
2. Revolted against Nebuchadnezzar (2 Kings 24:20)
3. Book of Acts is addressed to him (Acts 1:1)
5. Father of John the Baptist (Luke 1:5-23)
6. Sometimes known as the doubter (John 20:24-29)
8. Ninth of the minor prophets (Zeph. 1:1)

BIBLE CHARACTER CROSSWORD

ACROSS

1. Author of third and fifth New Testament books
3. A Gentile business woman, seller of purple; led to Christ by Paul
4. The eleventh and favorite son of Jacob
6. The son of King Saul who was David's good friend
7. Grandmother of Timothy
8. The prophet swallowed by a great fish
10. Author of twenty-sixth New Testament book
11. An apostle who was sometimes called "the Zealot"
12. Leader of Israel after Moses

DOWN

1. Father of Leah and Rachel
2. Third son of Leah and Jacob, and father of the tribe of priests
3. Brother of Mary and Martha raised from the dead by Jesus
4. Apostle who betrayed Jesus
5. Abraham's nephew
6. King of Judah and father of King Ahaz
8. Good king of Judah who had the temple repaired
9. First wife of Jacob

If you need help, you may use a concordance or Bible dictionary.

33

BIBLE CHARACTER CROSSWORD

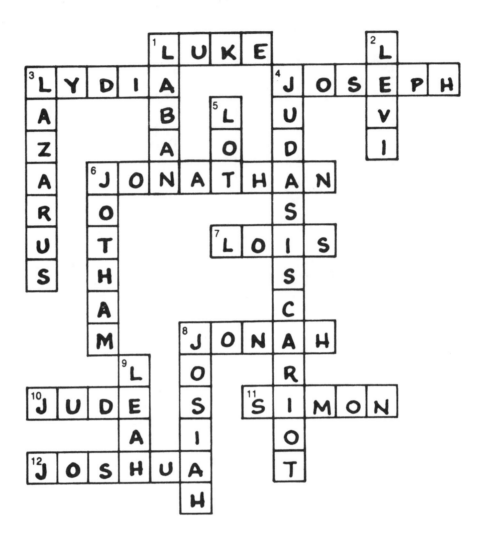

ACROSS
1. Author of third and fifth New Testament books
3. A Gentile business woman, seller of purple; led to Christ by Paul
4. The eleventh and favorite son of Jacob
6. The son of King Saul who was David's good friend
7. Grandmother of Timothy
8. The prophet swallowed by a great fish
10. Author of twenty-sixth New Testament book
11. An apostle who was sometimes called "the Zealot"
12. Leader of Israel after Moses

DOWN
1. Father of Leah and Rachel
2. Third son of Leah and Jacob, and father of the tribe of priests
3. Brother of Mary and Martha raised from the dead by Jesus
4. Apostle who betrayed Jesus
5. Abraham's nephew
6. King of Judah and father of King Ahaz
8. Good king of Judah who had the temple repaired
9. First wife of Jacob

34

2
OLD AND NEW TESTAMENT CROSSWORDS

MOSES CROSSWORD PUZZLE

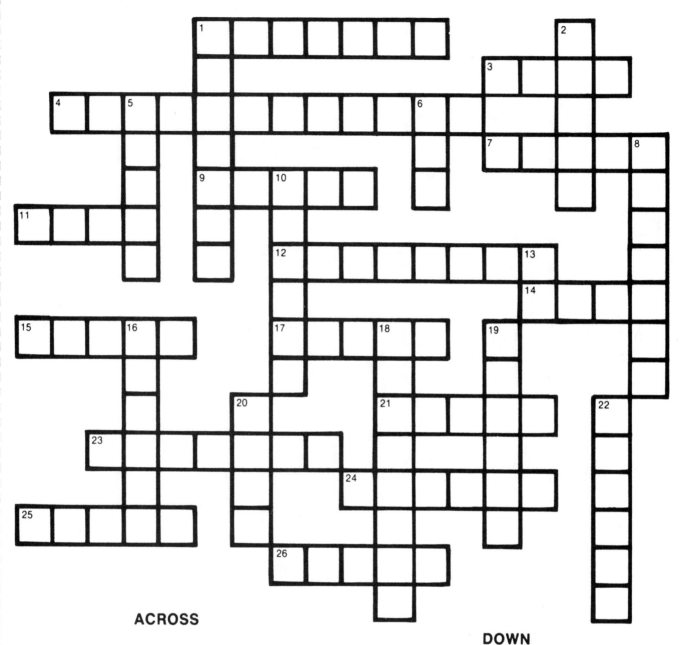

ACROSS

1. God sent ten _____ on the Egyptians.
3. Aaron helped build the golden _____.
4. Moses received the ten _____.
7. Second plague. Exod. 8:5.
9. Brother of Moses.
11. Third plague. Exod. 8:16.
12. Ninth plague. Exod. 10:21.
14. A pillar of _____ led them at night.
15. Plague after the murrain. Exod. 9:9.
17. The land of captivity.
21. Mount where Moses received the law.
23. Plague after flies. Exod. 9:3.
24. Where Israelites lived. Exod. 8:22.
25. The last plague brought _____ to the firstborn of Egypt.
26. The fourth plague. Exod. 8:21.

DOWN

1. Ruler of Egypt. Exod. 8:1.
2. Water was changed to _____. Exod. 7:19.
5. Leader of Israelites.
6. Number of commandments.
8. Moses' rod turned to a _____.
10. Body of water which was crossed by the Israelites.
13. Abbreviation of San Francisco.
16. Plague after hail. Exod. 10:4.
18. The Jewish feast of the _____ began in Egypt.
19. The Israelites were _____ in Egypt.
20. Plague after boils. Exod. 9:22.
22. Leader of Israel after Moses.

MOSES CROSSWORD PUZZLE

ACROSS

1. God sent ten _____ on the Egyptians.
3. Aaron helped build the golden _____.
4. Moses received the ten _____.
7. Second plague. Exod. 8:5.
9. Brother of Moses.
11. Third plague. Exod. 8:16.
12. Ninth plague. Exod. 10:21.
14. A pillar of _____ led them at night.
15. Plague after the murrain. Exod. 9:9.
17. The land of captivity.
21. Mount where Moses received the law.
23. Plague after flies. Exod. 9:3.
24. Where Israelites lived. Exod. 8:22.
25. The last plague brought _____ to the firstborn of Egypt.
26. The fourth plague. Exod. 8:21.

DOWN

1. Ruler of Egypt. Exod. 8:1.
2. Water was changed to _____. Exod. 7:19.
5. Leader of Israelites.
6. Number of commandments.
8. Moses' rod turned to a _____.
10. Body of water which was crossed by the Israelites.
13. Abbreviation of San Francisco.
16. Plague after hail. Exod. 10:4.
18. The Jewish feast of the _____ began in Egypt.
19. The Israelites were _____ in Egypt.
20. Plague after boils. Exod. 9:22.
22. Leader of Israel after Moses.

NEW TESTAMENT BOOKS

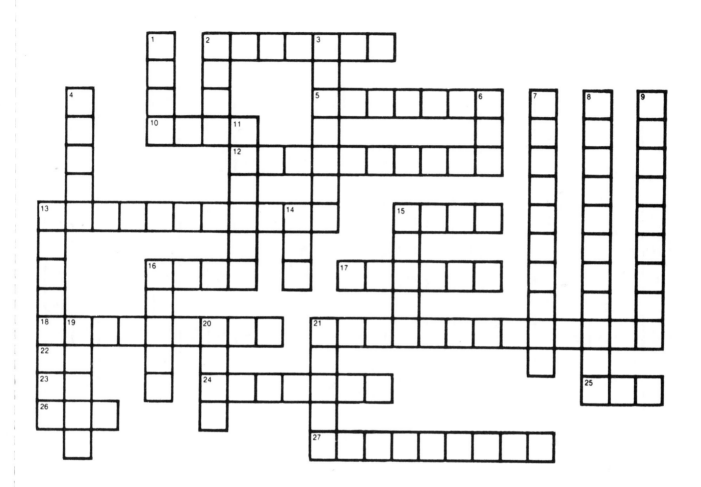

ACROSS

2. First book of New Testament.
5. When we hear, we must _ _ _ _ _ _ _.
10. Third book of New Testament.
12. Last book of Bible.
13. Book following Ephesians.
15. Fourth book of New Testament.
16. Book before Revelation.
17. Book following Acts.
18. Book after Galatians.
21. Book following Colossians.
22. Short for myself.
23. Abbreviation for Old Testament.
24. Book before Titus.
25. What we must not do. (Romans 6:6b)
26. The _ _ _ Testament.
27. Christ offers us _ _ _ _ _ _ _ _ _-
    _ (Acts 4:12)

DOWN

1. Writer of Romans.
2. Second book of New Testament.
3. Book after Philemon.
4. Another name for belief.
6. Long period of time.
7. Twelfth book of New Testament.
8. Book after Romans.
9. Ninth book of New Testament.
11. A weasel whose fur is used in garments.
13. Book after Titus.
14. The _ _ _ Testament.
15. Book after Hebrews.
16. Son of God.
19. Book after James.
20. Fifth book of New Testament.
21. Book before Philemon.

NEW TESTAMENT BOOKS

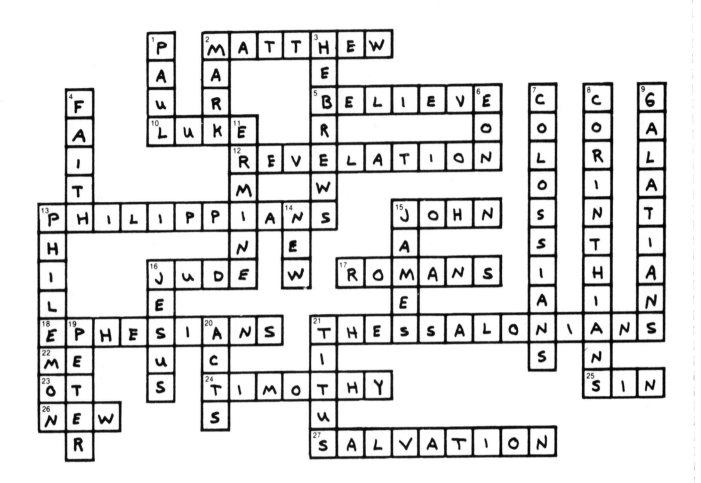

ACROSS

2. First book of New Testament.
5. When we hear, we must _ _ _ _ _ _.
10. Third book of New Testament.
12. Last book of Bible.
13. Book following Ephesians.
15. Fourth book of New Testament.
16. Book before Revelation.
17. Book following Acts.
18. Book after Galatians.
21. Book following Colossians.
22. Short for myself.
23. Abbreviation for Old Testament.
24. Book before Titus.
25. What we must not do. (Romans 6:6b)
26. The _ _ _ Testament.
27. Christ offers us _ _ _ _ _ _ _ _ _ _.
    _ _ (Acts 4:12)

DOWN

1. Writer of Romans.
2. Second book of New Testament.
3. Book after Philemon.
4. Another name for belief.
6. Long period of time.
7. Twelfth book of New Testament.
8. Book after Romans.
9. Ninth book of New Testament.
11. A weasel whose fur is used in garments.
13. Book after Titus.
14. The _ _ _ Testament.
15. Book after Hebrews.
16. Son of God.
19. Book after James.
20. Fifth book of New Testament.
21. Book before Philemon.

40

SERMON ON THE MOUNT

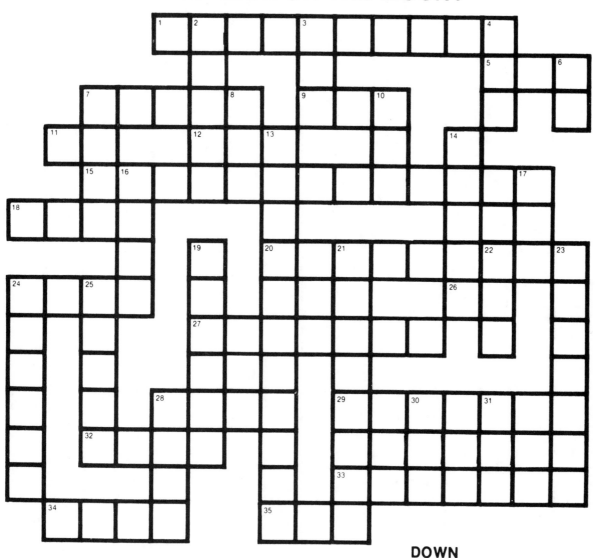

Matthew, Chapter 5

ACROSS

1. Blessed are they which are _____. (vs. 10)
5. Opposite of even.
7. Blessed are they that _____. (vs. 4)
9. A beam of light.
11. Opposite of stop.
12. Opposite of bottom.
15. We should hunger after _____. (vs. 6)
18. We have these on our feet.
20. Those that mourn shall be _____. (vs. 4)
24. Ye are the _____ of the earth. (vs. 13)
26. He went _____ the store.
27. A symbol for a number is a _____.
28. The _____ shall inherit the earth. (vs. 5)
29. What the meek will do. (vs. 5)
32. A drop of moisture from the eye.
33. Wild, or not tamed.
34. Blessed are _____ that mourn. (vs. 4)
35. Short for Sally.

DOWN

2. What the meek will inherit. (vs. 5)
3. What you hear with.
4. A female deer.
6. You should always _____ what's right.
7. _____ or less.
8. Think _____ that I am come to destroy. (vs. 17)
10. Opposite of no.
13. _____ are called the children of God. (vs. 9)
14. Blessed are the pure in _____. (vs. 8)
16. Contraction of is and not.
17. You _____ with your eyes.
19. We should _____ and thirst after righteousness. (vs. 6)
21. Who shall obtain mercy? (vs. 7)
22. Short for Thomas.
23. The wood _____ in with the tide.
24. Blessed are the poor in _____. (vs. 3)
25. Ye are the _____ of the world. (vs. 14)
28. Mother of Jesus.
30. Opposite of cold.
31. A male sheep.

SERMON ON THE MOUNT

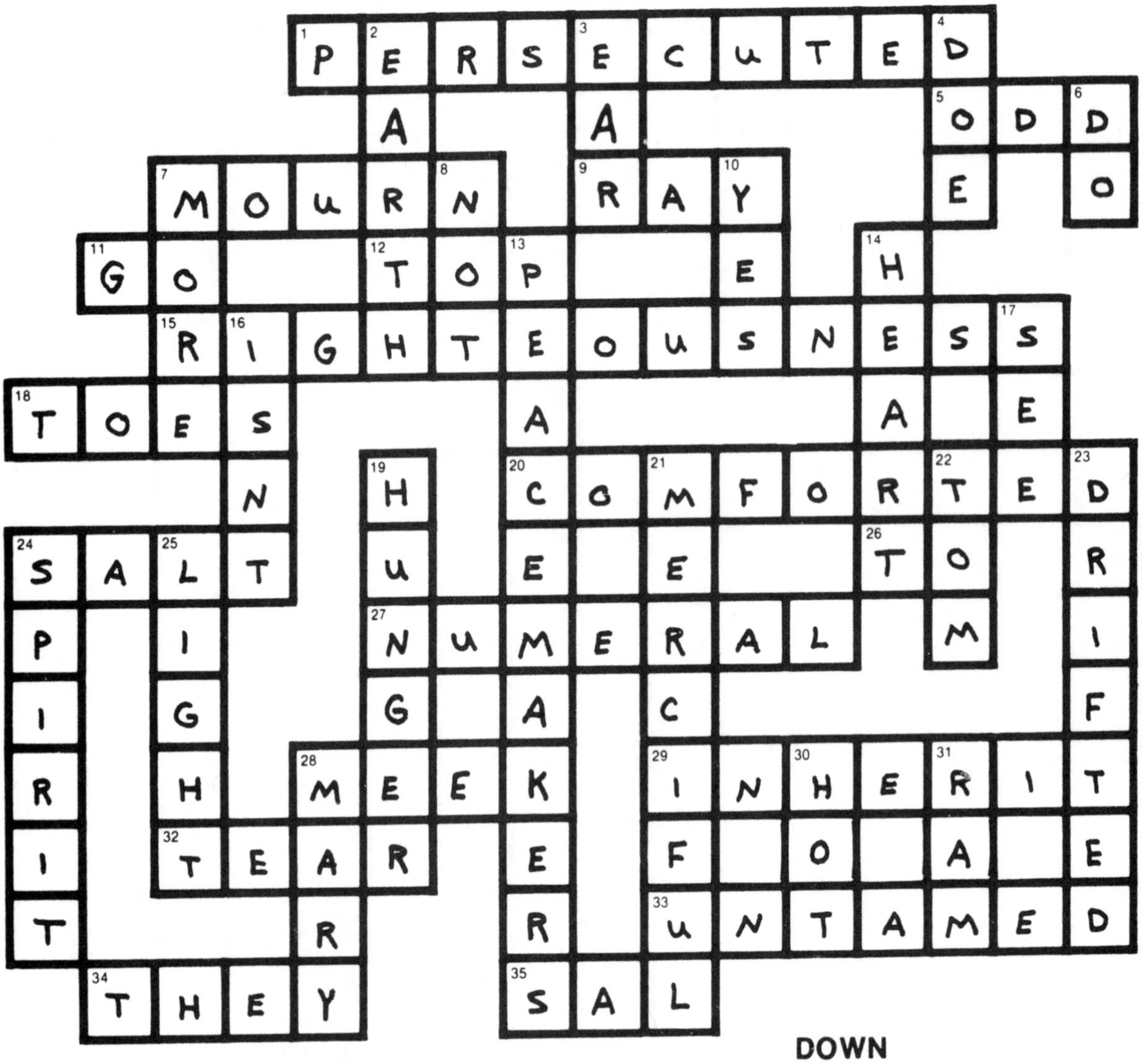

The completed crossword grid reads:

Across: 1 PERSECUTED, 5 ODD, 7 MOURN, 9 RAY, 11 GO, 12 TOP, 15 RIGHTEOUSNESS, 18 TOES, 20 COMFORTED, 24 SALT, 26 TO, 27 NUMERAL, 28 MEEK, 29 INHERIT, 32 TEAR, 33 UNTAMED, 34 THEY, 35 SAL

Down: 2 EARTH, 3 EAR, 4 DOE, 6 DO, 8 NOT, 10 YES, 13 PEACEMAKERS, 14 HEART, 16 ISN'T, 17 SEE, 19 HUNGER, 21 MERCIFUL, 22 TOM, 23 DRIFT, 24 SPIRIT, 25 LIGHT, 28 MARY, 30 HOT, 31 RAM

Matthew, Chapter 5

ACROSS

1. Blessed are they which are _____. (vs. 10)
5. Opposite of even.
7. Blessed are they that _____. (vs. 4)
9. A beam of light.
11. Opposite of stop.
12. Opposite of bottom.
15. We should hunger after _____. (vs. 6)
18. We have these on our feet.
20. Those that mourn shall be _____. (vs. 4)
24. Ye are the _____ of the earth. (vs. 13)
26. He went _____ the store.
27. A symbol for a number is a _____.
28. The _____ shall inherit the earth. (vs. 5)
29. What the meek will do. (vs. 5)
32. A drop of moisture from the eye.
33. Wild, or not tamed.
34. Blessed are _____ that mourn. (vs. 4)
35. Short for Sally.

DOWN

2. What the meek will inherit. (vs. 5)
3. What you hear with.
4. A female deer.
6. You should always _____ what's right.
7. _____ or less.
8. Think _____ that I am come to destroy. (vs. 17)
10. Opposite of no.
13. _____ are called the children of God. (vs. 9)
14. Blessed are the pure in _____. (vs. 8)
16. Contraction of is and not.
17. You _____ with your eyes.
19. We should _____ and thirst after righteousness. (vs. 6)
21. Who shall obtain mercy? (vs. 7)
22. Short for Thomas.
23. The wood _____ in with the tide.
24. Blessed are the poor in _____. (vs. 3)
25. Ye are the _____ of the world. (vs. 14)
28. Mother of Jesus.
30. Opposite of cold.
31. A male sheep.

BIBLE PUZZLES
PUZZLES
CROSSWORDS

3
BIBLE FILL-UPS

24 I	10 S	A	I	A	H		16 H
23 H	A	15 G	G	A	I		I
E	X	5 O	3 D	9 U	S		
J	U	8 D	1 G	E	11 S		

L	A	M	E	N	12 T	A	17 T	I	13 O	21 N	S

P	R	27 O	6 V	E	R	B	S	26 S

28 N	14 U	M	B	7 E	R	S

P	S	A	L	4 M	S	25 S

22 D	A	N	I	E	20 L

H	2 O	19 S	E	A

A	M	18 O	S

OLD TESTAMENT FILL-UP

Use the letters that are given to help you fill in all the Old Testament books listed below. Better use a pencil — you may have to move some books around before you get them all in the correct places!

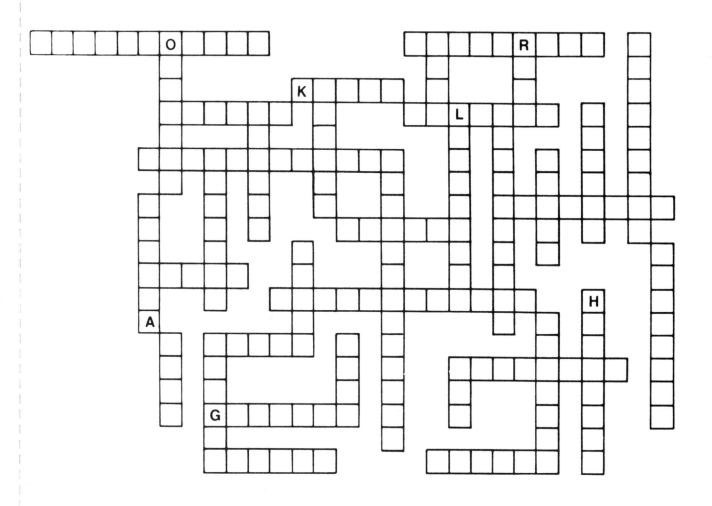

GENESIS	NEHEMIAH	HOSEA
EXODUS	ESTHER	JOEL
LEVITICUS	JOB	AMOS
NUMBERS	PSALMS	OBADIAH
DEUTERONOMY	PROVERBS	JONAH
JOSHUA	ECCLESIASTES	MICAH
JUDGES	SONG OF SOLOMON	NAHUM
RUTH	ISAIAH	HABAKKUK
SAMUEL	JEREMIAH	ZEPHANIAH
KINGS	LAMENTATIONS	HAGGAI
CHRONICLES	EZEKIEL	ZECHARIAH
EZRA	DANIEL	MALACHI

OLD TESTAMENT FILL-UP

Use the letters that are given to help you fill in all the Old Testament books listed below. Better use a pencil — you may have to move some books around before you get them all in the correct places!

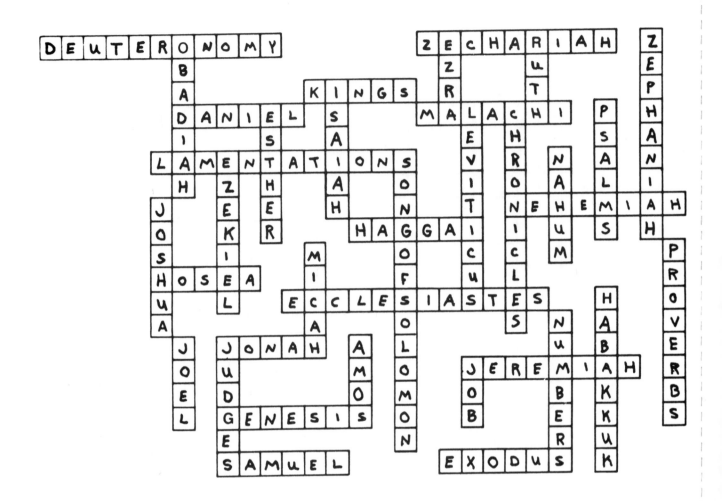

GENESIS	NEHEMIAH	HOSEA
EXODUS	ESTHER	JOEL
LEVITICUS	JOB	AMOS
NUMBERS	PSALMS	OBADIAH
DEUTERONOMY	PROVERBS	JONAH
JOSHUA	ECCLESIASTES	MICAH
JUDGES	SONG OF SOLOMON	NAHUM
RUTH	ISAIAH	HABAKKUK
SAMUEL	JEREMIAH	ZEPHANIAH
KINGS	LAMENTATIONS	HAGGAI
CHRONICLES	EZEKIEL	ZECHARIAH
EZRA	DANIEL	MALACHI

NEW TESTAMENT FILL-UP

Start with Matthew and add each of the New Testament books below until the entire puzzle is complete. Better use a pencil—you may have to move some books around before you get them all in the correct places!

MATTHEW	EPHESIANS	JAMES
MARK	PHILIPPIANS	FIRST PETER
LUKE	COLOSSIANS	2 PETER
JOHN	THESSALONIANS	FIRST JOHN
ACTS	TIMOTHY	SECOND JOHN
ROMANS	TITUS	3 JOHN
CORINTHIANS	PHILEMON	JUDE
GALATIANS	HEBREWS	REVELATION

NEW TESTAMENT FILL-UP

Start with Matthew and add each of the New Testament books below until the entire puzzle is complete. Better use a pencil—you may have to move some books around before you get them all in the correct places!

MATTHEW
MARK
LUKE
JOHN
ACTS
ROMANS
CORINTHIANS
GALATIANS

EPHESIANS
PHILIPPIANS
COLOSSIANS
THESSALONIANS
TIMOTHY
TITUS
PHILEMON
HEBREWS

JAMES
FIRST PETER
2 PETER
FIRST JOHN
SECOND JOHN
3 JOHN
JUDE
REVELATION

NEW TESTAMENT FINISH-IT

Use the letters that are given to help you fill in all the New Testament books below. Fill in books only as you begin to get clues from various letters.

MATTHEW	GALATIANS	PHILEMON
MARK	EPHESIANS	HEBREWS
LUKE	PHILIPPIANS	JAMES
JOHN	COLOSSIANS	PETER
ACTS	THESSALONIANS	1 JOHN
ROMANS	TIMOTHY	JUDE
CORINTHIANS	TITUS	REVELATION

NEW TESTAMENT FINISH-IT

Use the letters that are given to help you fill in all the New Testament books below. Fill in books only as you begin to get clues from various letters.

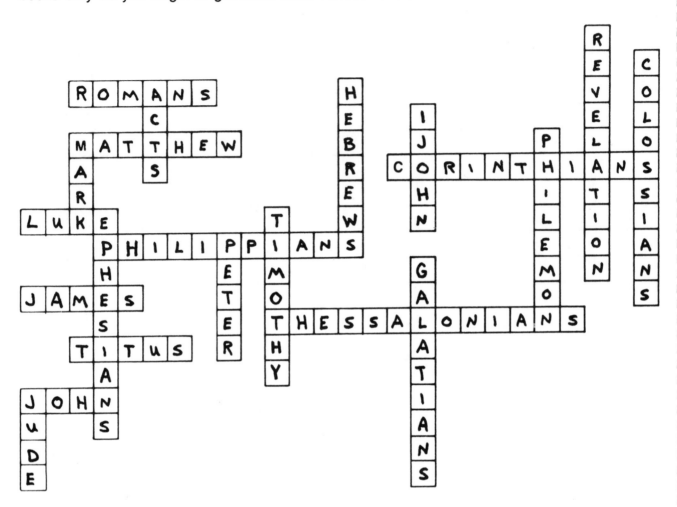

MATTHEW	GALATIANS	PHILEMON
MARK	EPHESIANS	HEBREWS
LUKE	PHILIPPIANS	JAMES
JOHN	COLOSSIANS	PETER
ACTS	THESSALONIANS	1 JOHN
ROMANS	TIMOTHY	JUDE
CORINTHIANS	TITUS	REVELATION

OLD TESTAMENT MATCH THE MESSAGE

Fill in the squares and transfer the letters to the matching squares below. You will read an important message.

The book following Song of Solomon

The book before Zechariah

Second book of the Bible

Seventh book of the Old Testament

Twenty-fifth book of Bible

The sixth book before Ezekiel

The fourth book before Ruth

The first book to begin with "P"

The book twelve back from Malachi

The book before Joel

The book before Obadiah

1	2	3	4	5	6	7	8	9	10	11	12	13	14	15	16

17	18	19	20	21	22	23	24	25	26	27	28

OLD TESTAMENT MATCH THE MESSAGE

Fill in the squares and transfer the letters to the matching squares below. You will read an important message.

The book following Song of Solomon

The book before Zechariah

Second book of the Bible

Seventh book of the Old Testament

Twenty-fifth book of Bible

The sixth book before Ezekiel

The fourth book before Ruth

The first book to begin with "P"

The book twelve back from Malachi

The book before Joel

The book before Obadiah

I(24)	S(10)	A	I	A	H(16)	

H(23)	A	G(15)	G	A	I
E	X	O(5)	D(3)	U(9)	S
J	U	D(8)	G(1)	E(11)	S

L	A	M	E	N(12)	T	A	T(17)	I	O(13)	N(21)	S
				P	R	O(27)	V(6)	E	R	B	S(26)
					N(28)	U(14)	M	B	E	R(7)	S
						P	S	A	L(4)	M	S(25)
						D(22)	A	N	I	E(20)	L
							H	O(2)	S(19)	E	A
								A	M	O(18)	S

1	2	3	4	5	6	7	8	9	10	11	12	13	14	15	16
G	O	D	L	O	V	E	D	U	S	E	N	O	U	G	H

17	18	19	20	21	22	23	24	25	26	27	28
T	O	S	E	N	D	H	I	S	S	O	N

52

NEW TESTAMENT MATCH THE MESSAGE

Fill in the squares above and transfer the letters to the matching squares below. You will read an important message.

The book before Ephesians

The book which is three before Romans

The fourth book after 1 John

The book before Revelation

The seventh book of the New Testament

The book which is four before Acts

The seventh book after Acts

The eleventh book of the New Testament

The fifth book after Acts

The thirteenth New Testament book

1	2	3	4	5	6	7	8	9	10	11	12	13

14	15	16	17	18	19	20	21	22	23	24

NEW TESTAMENT MATCH THE MESSAGE

Fill in the squares above and transfer the letters to the matching squares below. You will read an important message.

The book before Ephesians

| 10 G | A | 24 L | A | T | I | A | N | S |

The book which is three before Romans

| L | U | 4 K | E |

The fourth book after 1 John

| R | E | 22 V | E | L | A | 18 T | I | 11 O | N |

The book before Revelation

| J | 16 U | 13 D | 9 E |

The seventh book of the New Testament

| C | 2 O | R | I | N | T | 15 H | I | A | N | S |

The book which is four before Acts

| M | A | 5 T | T | 19 H | E | W |

The seventh book after Acts

| C | 3 O | L | 12 O | S | S | I | A | N | S |

The eleventh book of the New Testament

| P | 8 H | I | 1 L | I | P | P | I | A | 17 N | S |

The fifth book after Acts

| 20 E | P | H | E | S | 23 I | A | N | S |

The thirteenth New Testament book

| 7 T | H | 21 E | S | S | A | L | 6 O | N | I | A | N | 14 S |

1	2	3	4	5	6	7	8	9	10	11	12	13
L	O	O	K	T	O	T	H	E	G	O	O	D

14	15	16	17	18	19	20	21	22	23	24
S	H	U	N	T	H	E	E	V	I	L

SEEK AND FIND

Fill in the squares above and transfer the letters to the matching squares below. You will read an important message.

The book following 3 John

The book following Matthew

The book before Colossians

The book before James

The book after Jude

The book before 1 Corinthians

The book after Titus

The book before Romans

The book before Ephesians

The book after Luke

The book before Mark

Grid (upper):

		10	3	
			14	17
12			22				31	23
			21	18		16	
	25		8		27	4	
					28		5
20			19	29	2	
			9		6	
1				11			26
			13	
		32	24	7	30	15

1	2	3	4	5	6	7	8	9	10	11	12	13	14

15	16	17	18	19	20	21	22	23	24	25	26	27	28	29	30	31	32

55

SEEK AND FIND

Fill in the squares above and transfer the letters to the matching squares below. You will read an important message.

The book following 3 John

The book following Matthew

The book before Colossians

The book before James

The book after Jude

The book before 1 Corinthians

The book after Titus

The book before Romans

The book before Ephesians

The book after Luke

The book before Mark

JU D(10) E(3)

M A R(14) K(17)

P H(12) I L I(22) P P I A N(31) S(23)

H(21) E(18) B R E(16) W S

R E(25) V E(8) L A T(27) I(4) O N

R O M A N(28) S(5)

P(20) H I L E(19) M(29) O(2) N

A(9) C T(6) S

G(1) A L A T(11) I A N S(26)

J O(13) H N

M A(32) T(24) T(7) H E(30) W(15)

1	2	3	4	5	6	7	8	9	10	11	12	13	14
G	O	D	I	S	T	H	E	A	U	T	H	O	R

15	16	17	18	19	20	21	22	23	24	25	26	27	28	29	30	31	32
W	E	K	E	E	P	H	I	S	T	E	S	T	A	M	E	N	T

56

OLD TESTAMENT SOLVE-IT

Find the book of the Bible before (–) or after (+) the book shown below. Print the word below the problem in the box with that Bible book. Then read the message shown. For example, 4 books after Genesis is Deuteronomy. Print CRIME in the Deuteronomy box.

Lamentations	**Jeremiah**	**Job**	**Isaiah**
Deuteronomy	**Amos**	**I Chronicles**	**Proverbs**
, **Malachi**	**Psalms**	**Daniel**	**Ecclesiastes**
Ezekiel	**Nahum**	**Joel**	? **Habakkuk**

Genesis
+ 4
CRIME

Ruth
+ 5
BE

1 Kings
+ 8
COULD

Ezra
+ 9
IT

Esther
+ 6
A

Psalms
+ 6
IF

Proverbs
+ 10
TO

Isaiah
+ 4
EVIDENCE

Jeremiah
– 3
BE

Ezekiel
– 6
A

Daniel
– 9
WERE

Micah
– 4
CONVICT

Joel
+ 5
TO

Amos
– 4
FOUND

Jonah
+ 7
CHRISTIAN

Malachi
– 4
YOU

OLD TESTAMENT SOLVE-IT

Find the book of the Bible before (−) or after (+) the book shown below. Print the word below the problem in the box with that Bible book. Then read the message shown. For example, 4 books after Genesis is Deuteronomy. Print CRIME in the Deuteronomy box.

IF	IT	WERE	A
Lamentations	Jeremiah	Job	Isaiah
CRIME	TO	BE	A
Deuteronomy	Amos	I Chronicles	Proverbs
CHRISTIAN,	COULD	EVIDENCE	BE
Malachi	Psalms	Daniel	Ecclesiastes
FOUND	TO	CONVICT	YOU?
Ezekiel	Nahum	Joel	Habakkuk

Genesis	Ruth	1 Kings	Ezra	Esther
+ 4	+ 5	+ 8	+ 9	+ 6
CRIME	**BE**	**COULD**	**IT**	**A**

Psalms	Proverbs	Isaiah	Jeremiah	Ezekiel
+ 6	+ 10	+ 4	− 3	− 6
IF	**TO**	**EVIDENCE**	**BE**	**A**

Daniel	Micah	Joel	Amos	Jonah
− 9	− 4	+ 5	− 4	+ 7
WERE	**CONVICT**	**TO**	**FOUND**	**CHRISTIAN**

Malachi
− 4
YOU

NEW TESTAMENT SOLVE-IT

Find the book of the Bible before (−) or after (+) the book shown below. Print the word below the problem in the box with that Bible book. Then read the message shown. For example, 6 books after Matthew is I Corinthians. Print LET in the I Corinthians box.

1 Corinthians	1 Thessalonians	Ephesians	James	Colossians
Galatians	1 Timothy	2 Corinthians	Revelation	2 John ,
Hebrews	John	Philemon	2 Thessalonians	Jude
Philippians	Matthew	Acts	Romans	Titus

Matthew
+ 6
LET

Mark
+ 7
WHO

Luke
+ 16
AND

Galatians
− 8
WELL

1 Corinthians
+ 8
ARE

Acts
+ 8
US

Philemon
− 4
PEOPLE

Hebrews
− 13
TO

2 Timothy
+ 4
AS

1 Thessalonians
− 8
PREPARED

1 Timothy
− 5
LIVE

John
+ 7
ARE

1 Peter
− 9
PEOPLE

Jude
− 9
LIVE

2 Corinthians
− 4
DIE

Philippians
− 3
PREPARED

2 Peter
+ 2
DIE

Colossians
+ 6
AS

1 John
+ 3
WHO

Titus
+ 10
TO

NEW TESTAMENT SOLVE-IT

Find the book of the Bible before (–) or after (+) the book shown below. Print the word below the problem in the box with that Bible book. Then read the message shown. For example, 6 books after Matthew is I Corinthians. Print LET in the I Corinthians box.

LET	US	LIVE	AS	PEOPLE
1 Corinthians	1 Thessalonians	Ephesians	James	Colossians
WHO	**ARE**	**PREPARED**	**TO**	**DIE,**
Galatians	1 Timothy	2 Corinthians	Revelation	2 John
AND	**DIE**	**AS**	**PEOPLE**	**WHO**
Hebrews	John	Philemon	2 Thessalonians	Jude
ARE	**WELL**	**PREPARED**	**TO**	**LIVE**
Philippians	Matthew	Acts	Romans	Titus

Matthew	Mark	Luke	Galatians	1 Corinthians	Acts
+ 6	+ 7	+ 16	– 8	+ 8	+ 8
LET	**WHO**	**AND**	**WELL**	**ARE**	**US**

Philemon	Hebrews	2 Timothy	1 Thessalonians	1 Timothy	John
– 4	– 13	+ 4	– 8	– 5	+ 7
PEOPLE	**TO**	**AS**	**PREPARED**	**LIVE**	**ARE**

1 Peter	Jude	2 Corinthians	Philippians	2 Peter	Colossians
– 9	– 9	– 4	– 3	+ 2	+ 6
PEOPLE	**LIVE**	**DIE**	**PREPARED**	**DIE**	**AS**

1 John	Titus
+ 3	+ 10
WHO	**TO**